pop stand

Arranged by Brent Edstrom

contents

ISBN 978-1-4950-5166-1

HAL•LEONARD®
CORPORATION
7777 W. BLUEMOUND RD. P.O. BOX 13819 MILWAUKEE, WI 53213

Visit Hal Leonard Online at
www.halleonard.com

BRIDGE OVER TROUBLED WATER

Words and Music by
PAUL SIMON

CALIFORNIA DREAMIN'

Words and Music by JOHN PHILLIPS
and MICHELLE PHILLIPS

8

EVERY BREATH YOU TAKE

Music and Lyrics by
STING

Moderate Swing

FIFTY WAYS TO LEAVE YOUR LOVER

Words and Music by
PAUL SIMON

Bright Swing Waltz

18

20

GOD ONLY KNOWS

Words and Music by BRIAN WILSON
and TONY ASHER

HAPPY TOGETHER

Words and Music by GARRY BONNER
and ALAN GORDON

HOW DEEP IS YOUR LOVE

from the Motion Picture SATURDAY NIGHT FEVER

Words and Music by BARRY GIBB,
ROBIN GIBB and MAURICE GIBB

I'M NOT IN LOVE

Words and Music by ERIC STEWART
and GRAHAM GOULDMAN

34

IMAGINE

Words and Music by
JOHN LENNON

THE LOOK OF LOVE

from CASINO ROYALE

Words by HAL DAVID
Music by BURT BACHARACH

JUST THE WAY YOU ARE

Words and Music by
BILLY JOEL

LEAN ON ME

Words and Music by
BILL WITHERS

MAN IN THE MIRROR

Words and Music by GLEN BALLARD
and SIEDAH GARRETT

SORRY SEEMS TO BE THE HARDEST WORD

Words and Music by ELTON JOHN
and BERNIE TAUPIN

MOONDANCE

Words and Music by
VAN MORRISON

Moderate Swing

64

PEOPLE GET READY

Words and Music by
CURTIS MAYFIELD

RED, RED WINE

Words and Music by
NEIL DIAMOND

SAVE THE LAST DANCE FOR ME

Words and Music by DOC POMUS
and MORT SHUMAN

STAND BY ME

Words and Music by JERRY LIEBER,
MIKE STOLLER and BEN E. KING

Medium New Orleans groove

TEARS IN HEAVEN

Words and Music by ERIC CLAPTON
and WILL JENNINGS

84

87

TIME AFTER TIME

Words and Music by CYNDI LAUPER
and ROB HYMAN

Flowing Latin groove

WE'VE ONLY JUST BEGUN

Words and Music by ROGER NICHOLS
and PAUL WILLIAMS

WITH A LITTLE HELP FROM MY FRIENDS

Words and Music by JOHN LENNON
and PAUL McCARTNEY